Asteroid Alarm!

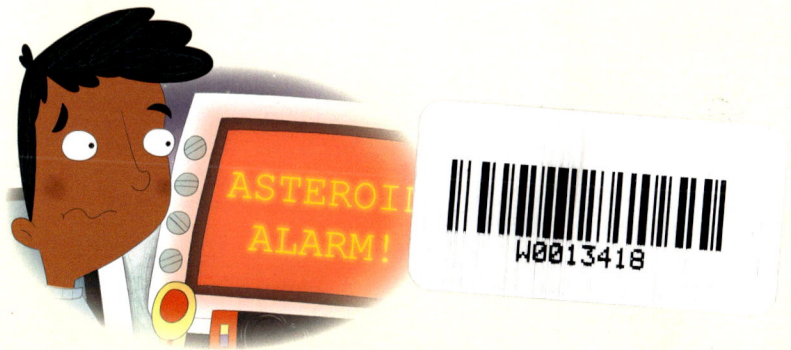

Written by Adam and Charlotte Guillain

Chapter 1: Into Space

Rav's mum and dad were taking him and his friends to Planet Zoom. They stopped at the gift shop on the way in.

"I'm going to buy a rubber for my summer challenge," said Finn. Their teacher had asked them to collect six objects over the holidays.

"Let's go to the new planetarium!" said Rav, as they left the shop.

"They show a film that makes it feel like you're zooming around the solar system!" Rav explained, leading the way into the planetarium and finding four empty seats.

The room went dark and stars twinkled on the ceiling overhead. Then a huge cinema screen lit up and the friends felt as if they were flying through space.

The film made it seem like they were shooting up from Earth towards the Moon.

Then Finn cried out, "Is my seat supposed to tip backwards?" and he gripped the arms.

"No!" said Asha. "I think we're going into space for real!"

The friends closed their eyes as the roar of engines rang out around them.

When the roaring noise had stopped, Finn relaxed his grip and peered around. His friends were sitting alongside him, all staring with wide eyes.

"We're on some sort of spaceship!" said Tess, running her hands over the flashing control panel in front of them.

"But where are we?" asked Rav, leaning forward in his seat.

"Isn't that the Moon?" said Finn, pointing up ahead.

"Yes!" said Asha. "And look behind you. There's Earth!"

They all spun around on their seats and gasped at the sight of the blue and green planet far below.

"I can see Africa!" shouted Tess.

"We're flying through the solar system for real," said Rav with a wide smile.

"I think we're heading towards Mars next!" said Finn, spinning back around and glimpsing a red planet getting closer and closer ahead of them.

"Wow, we're going very fast!" gulped Asha.

Chapter 2: Flying a Spaceship

Rav looked at the lights and dials on the control panel. He flicked a switch and a robotic voice spoke. Rav tilted his head to listen.

"This is the ship's computer. Would you like to take over the manual controls and fly the ship?"

Rav turned to grin at his friends.

"Are you sure that's a good idea, Rav?" asked Finn, his eyes darting over the complicated controls.

"It can't be any harder than the rides at Planet Zoom," murmured Rav. He touched the computer screen and a green light came on.

"Manual controls in operation," came the robotic voice.

Rav seized the controls and the others shot back in their seats as the ship lurched forwards. Rav felt a rush of excitement as he tilted the controls and felt the spaceship react.

"Let's take a proper look at Mars," he decided.

"How lovely and orange it is," said Asha. "Nothing like Earth."

"But it's so rocky and dry," added Tess with a shudder.
"Don't stop here, Rav."

"Okay," said Rav, pulling the controls back and shooting up
into space. "Where next?"

"Jupiter's the next planet," said Finn. "But I can't see it yet."

"Right," said Rav. "Hold on!"

The spaceship whooshed onwards, with the friends staring out of the windows looking for the next planet.

"Hang on!" cried Asha. "That doesn't look like Jupiter!"

"What can you see?" asked Tess, squinting into the blackness.

"Rocks!" shouted Asha. "Millions of them, and they're getting closer!"

"Stop, Rav! Turn around!" yelled Finn, as the rocks came hurtling towards them.

"I can't," Rav told him. "We're being pulled in!"

Tess put her hands over her eyes as the spaceship shot towards the danger. Asha grabbed Tess's arm and screamed, "Help!"

Chapter 3: Hit!

"Don't panic," said Rav calmly, as he gripped the controls and dodged the rocks whizzing all around. "I've got a computer game just like this. I've nearly completed it." He bit his lip and swerved around a particularly large rock.

"I can't look!" squeaked Tess.

Asha had spotted a chart on the wall. "I know what this is," she said. "These rocks are asteroids. We're in the asteroid belt between Mars and Jupiter!"

"How far is it to the other side?" asked Finn in a shaky voice.

"I don't know," replied Asha. "Hopefully not far!"

Luckily, the asteroids were clearing. "Well done, Rav!" Tess cheered, as the ship zoomed through the last of them.

CLUNK!

"What was that?" Finn said, looking at the back of the spaceship where the noise had come from.

"I think you cheered too soon, Tess," Rav said with a frown. "We just got hit!"

ASTEROID ALARM!

BEEP! BEEP! BEEP! A red light started to flash on the control panel, accompanied by a beeping sound much worse than a car alarm.

"Asteroid alarm! Asteroid alarm!" said the ship's computer. "We have been hit!"

"How bad is it?" Rav asked the computer.

The robotic voice replied immediately, "Engine damage! Send repair team to rear engine!"

"Repair team?" asked Tess. "Where are we going to find one of those?"

"I think we might be it," said Asha with a gulp.

ASTEROID ALARM!

Chapter 4: The Repair Team

Asha, Tess and Finn climbed out of their seats and hurried to the back of the ship.

"Do you need my help?" called Rav. He flicked the control switch he'd pressed earlier.

"Automatic controls not available," said the robotic computer. "Rear engine has been shut down. Please continue with manual controls."

"You'd better stay there!" said Finn.

"Repair team are in place," Rav told the computer. "What now?"

"Unscrew the silver panel!" the robotic voice replied.

"With what?" asked Finn, looking around in a panic.

Tess pulled open the drawers under the control panel and found a tool kit. "Here's a screwdriver!" she called.

With shaking hands, Tess carefully removed the screws and lifted off the panel. "Done!" she yelled.

"What next?" Rav asked.

"Find the unwanted object!" said the robotic voice.

"A piece of rock?" Asha wondered, peering inside the engine. "It's very dark in here!"

"Three minutes!" said the robotic voice. "The ship can only continue with one engine for three minutes. Please repair the rear engine immediately!"

Tess grabbed the tool kit, found a torch and shone it into the broken engine.

"I can see it!" she said.

"Quick!" shouted Rav, as more emergency lights began flashing on the control panel. "It's hard to control the ship with just one engine working!"

"I think I can reach it!" said Finn, stretching his fingers out.

"Got it!" he shouted, pulling out his hand and holding up a tiny piece of asteroid.

"Item removed," Rav told the ship's computer, sighing with relief.

But it wasn't over yet.

"Close the hole made by the unwanted object!" the robotic voice instructed.

Tess's face fell. "How are we going to do that?" she asked.

Finn felt his pockets, searching for something to help. He pulled out the rubber he'd bought at the theme park shop.

"This might work," he said, pushing it inside the engine. Finn pulled his arm out, but the flashing lights and beeping noise kept going.

"Hole closed!" Rav told the ship, but it didn't reply.

"HOLE CLOSED!" they all yelled together over the alarm. "HOLE CLOSED!"

The alarm stopped and the lights flashed out. The friends waited, not daring to breathe.

Chapter 5: Back to Planet Zoom

"Repair complete!" said the robotic voice. "Both engines are now working."

"You did it!" shouted Rav.

The friends collapsed into their seats.

"I'm still shaking!" said Tess.

Finn let out a deep breath.

"Look at that," whispered Asha, as she pointed out of the window.

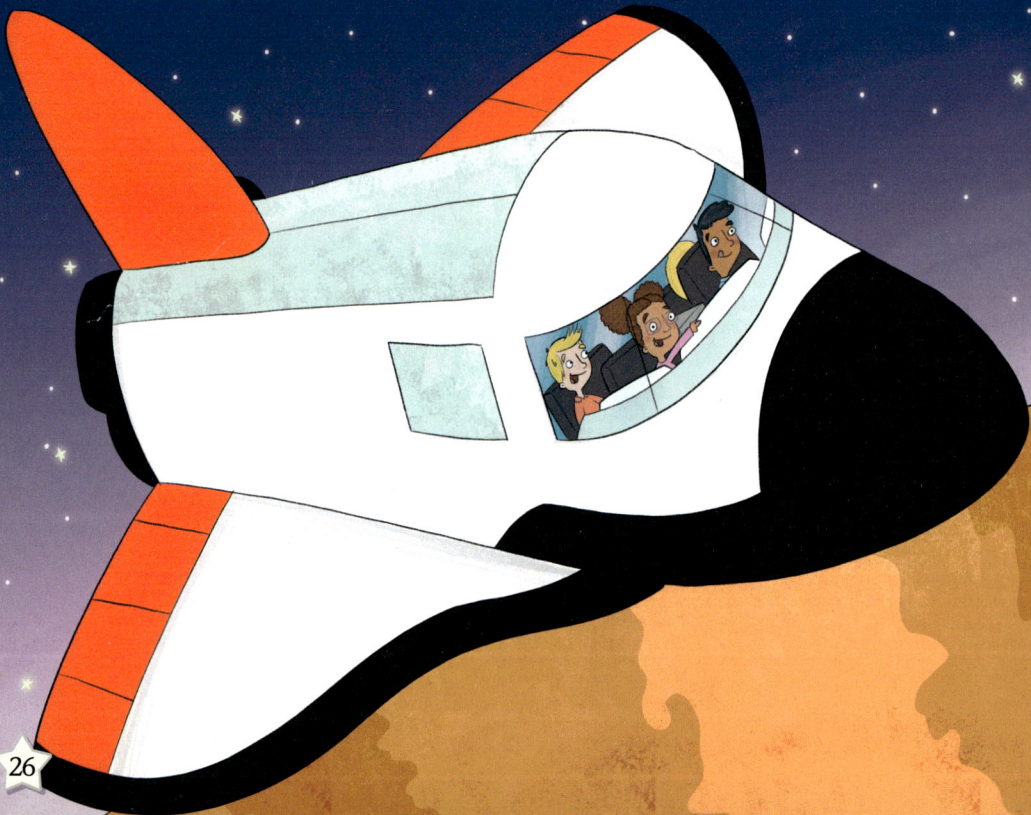

"Jupiter!" cried Rav. "It's huge!"

Soon the massive brownish-red and white planet was all they could see.

"It's amazing," murmured Tess.

They flew around Jupiter in silence, watching giant storm clouds swirling on the surface.

"Let's find some other planets," said Rav, pulling back the controls and shooting off into space once more.

"It must be Saturn next," thought Finn, but then he felt himself falling backwards.

"I think we're going back!" called Asha, as they were whirled away from the spaceship and back to Planet Zoom.

When they opened their eyes, everyone was leaving the planetarium.

As they walked out, Finn frowned. "I don't have the rubber for my summer challenge any more," he said.

"But you have something even better now, don't you?" said Asha.

Finn put his hand in his pocket. "The asteroid!" he said, holding it up as his friends crowded around to look.

Awesome!

Asteroid Alarm!

What other things will the Comet Street Kids collect
for their holiday challenge? Read the other books
in this band to find out!

Asteroid Alarm!

The Summer Fete

At the Seaside

The Laughing Kookaburra

Help the Vikings

The Sleepover

Talk about the story

Answer the questions:

1 What did Finn buy in the gift shop at Planet Zoom?

2 Which of Earth's continents did Tess spot from the spaceship?

3 How did Asha describe Mars?

4 What does the word 'glimpsing', on page 7, mean? Can you think of another word that has a similar meaning?

5 Why did Finn tell Rav to stay at the controls?

6 Why did they have to repair the rear engine quickly?

7 Can you describe how they fixed the engine in your own words?

8 Do you know any other stories or films that are set in space? Which is your favourite? Why?

Can you retell the story using your own words?